STAFFORDSHIRE LIBRARY AND INFORMATION SERVICES
Please return or renew by last date shown

WOMB

If not required by other readers this item may be renewed, in person, by post or by telephone. Please quote details above and due date for return. If issued by computer, the numbers on the barcode label on your ticket and on each item, together with date of return are required.

24HOUR RENEWAL LINE 0845 33 00 740

How life changed
in
Victorian
times

Dr Brian Knapp

▼ These figures give the total population for Great Britain and Ireland between 1570 and 1911. The Victorian period is shown between 1841 and 1901. The population grew rapidly over much of the Victorian period, but there was tragedy as well as success. In Ireland the population fell because of the potato famine.

Great Britain and Ireland

Year	population	growth %
1570	4.1	
1600	4.8	0.4
1630	5.6	0.5
1670	5.7	0.1
1700	6.0	0.2
1750	6.5	0.2

First census 1801 and every ten years after that

Year	population	growth %
1801	16.3	1.3
1811	18.5	1.2
1821	21.0	1.1
1831	24.1	1.8
1841	26.8	1.0
1851	27.5	0.2 *
1861	29.1	0.4
1871	31.6	0.8
1881	35.0	1.0
1891	37.8	0.7
1901	41.6	0.9
1911	45.4	0.9

* This low value is due to the population decline in Ireland as a result of the potato famine and emigration. The table below shows how Irish population was going down while the UK population as a whole was rising.

Ireland alone

year	population
1831	7.8
1841	8.2
1851	6.6
1861	5.8
1871	5.4
1881	5.2
1891	4.7
1901	4.4
1911	4.4

⚠ Look after our heritage!

It is easy to talk about looking after the environment, but we each have to help. Help is often small things, like being careful when you walk around old buildings, and not leaving scratch marks on anything that you visit. It doesn't take a lot of effort – just attitude.

Curriculum Visions

Curriculum Visions is a registered trademark of Atlantic Europe Publishing Company Ltd.

There's more on-line

There's more about other great Curriculum Visions packs and a wealth of supporting information available at our dedicated web site. Visit:

www.CurriculumVisions.com

✦ Atlantic Europe Publishing

First published in 2005 by
Atlantic Europe Publishing Company Ltd.
Copyright © 2005
Atlantic Europe Publishing Company Ltd.

Author
Brian Knapp, BSc, PhD

Art Director
Duncan McCrae, BSc

Senior Designer
Adele Humphries, BA, PGCE

Editor
Robert Anderson, BA, PGCE

Designed and produced by
EARTHSCAPE EDITIONS

Printed in China by
WKT Company Ltd

How life changed in Victorian times – *Curriculum Visions*
A CIP record for this book is available from the British Library

Paperback ISBN 1 86214 455 9
Hardback ISBN 1 86214 457 5

Illustrations (c=centre t=top b=bottom l=left r=right)
Mark Stacey cover, pages 6–7, 8–9, 10, 11, 18–19, 20–21, 22–23, 40–41; *David Woodroffe* pages 35, 37.

Picture credits
All photographs are from the Earthscape Editions photolibrary except the following: (c=centre t=top b=bottom l=left r=right)
Brighton Museum and Art Gallery page 32; *Esh Parish Council* page 36; *Mary Evans* pages 3, 9, 13t, 13b, 17t, 38, 39; *The Granger Collection, New York* pages 4, 12, 16, 28–29, 31; *Leeds Library and Information Services* pages 5, 27; *McCrae family collection* pages 1 and 25; *Roger Vaughan Picture Library* page 33; *Tunbridge Wells Museum and Art Gallery* page 24.

Acknowledgements
The publishers would like to thank David Croucher and those who supplied the images to Esh Parish Council.

This product is manufactured from sustainable managed forests. For every tree cut down at least one more is planted.

Contents

The Victorian age takes its name from Queen Victoria, who ruled Britain from 1837 to 1901. This photograph was taken in 1887 – the year of Queen Victoria's Golden Jubilee (her 50th year on the throne).

Words in **BOLD CAPITALS** are further explained in the glossary on page 47.

Who were the Victorians?

This book is about the VICTORIANS – people who lived during the long reign of Queen Victoria; from 1837 to 1901.

During Victorian times, Britain was called 'the workshop of the world' and it was at the centre of an empire larger than any other the world had known. On this page you will learn briefly about some of the changes that occurred during Victorian times.

▲ ① **This painting shows the Royal Family as it was in 1848. At the centre are Queen Victoria and Prince Albert surrounded by some of their children. In all, Victoria had nine children. Large families were common in Victorian times and lower death rates than in previous centuries led to a booming population.**

❶ During Victoria's reign the population of Great Britain almost doubled (picture ①).

❷ The Victorians lived at the end of the time called the **INDUSTRIAL REVOLUTION**. It was an exciting time of invention and huge change. The first metal ships, the **TELEGRAPH**, cheap steel-making, the camera, cinema, electric lamps and motors, and even the motor car, were all developed during Victorian times.

❸ The railway train was the single invention that most changed the lives of Victorians.

❹ Victorian society was strictly divided into **CLASSES**: upper class, middle class and working, or lower, class. Each class followed its own set of 'rules'.

❺ The government passed laws to improve the working and living conditions of poor people. As a result, people lived longer.

❻ The Victorians introduced schooling for all.

7 The Victorians were very proud of the **BRITISH EMPIRE**. The Empire helped make Britain rich because it was a source of goods and markets to sell products to.

8 During Victorian times millions of people moved from the countryside and into the expanding cities.

9 Although there was huge progress made for many people, some working people continued to live in poverty and squalor (picture ②).

10 Many famous writers, politicians, doctors and engineers lived in Victorian times. You can find out about some of them on pages 44–45.

▼ ② Although Britain and many of its people became richer during Victorian times, a large number of people still lived in poverty. This photograph shows a 'SLUM' in Leeds in about 1890. The building at the end on the right is the shared toilet (privvy) for all of the surrounding houses.

5

1837 – Early Victorian times

When Victoria came to the throne, life was fine for a small number of wealthy people, but grim for everyone else.

When Victoria came to the throne the Industrial Revolution was under way and people were leaving the countryside and looking for jobs in the cities.

▼ ① Here you can see some of the features of city life in Britain in early Victorian times. You can see what changes occurred by comparing it with the illustration on pages 40–41.

Visiting a city in 1837

Imagine visiting a city in 1837 (picture ①). As you approach the city, the first thing you see are lots of tall chimneys and the smoke belching out of them.

Most factories are close to river or canal and are being built right in the town centre.

Georgian squares elegant city houses for the wealthy

Brick-making factories

Textile mills with houses built close by

Market

Ironworks

River

Cottages where workers live

Old Tudor hall falling into ruin

However, the city isn't like the vast sprawling places we know today. It is quite small, and you can see the surrounding countryside.

On the outskirts of the city, there are cottages, just like those in the countryside, but there are also rows (terraces) of poorly built brick houses. Not far from these houses are the new factories with their giant chimneys.

Nearly everyone who works in the factories walks to work.

As you stroll between the houses and factories, you can hear the constant clatter of the machines inside the factories. Just beyond the grim-looking factory gates, hundreds of people are toiling away. As you cross a river or canal, you notice the barges of coal and other goods being pulled slowly by horses.

Near to the factory there is a great mansion. This belongs to the factory owner. The owner is proud of his factory and likes to be within sight of it. His managers also live in better houses than the workers, but only the owner has a horse and carriage.

The city centre still has some houses built during much older times, perhaps as long ago as the Tudor period. But there are also a few elegant streets and squares, built in **GEORGIAN** times. These are the homes of lawyers, doctors and other well-to-do people.

But as you wander around, little do you know how much this city is going to change in the coming decades…

Coal mines

Canal

Workhouse

A few Tudor and other early buildings survive.

Barges on rivers and canals are the main way of carrying goods about.

7

Children at work

If you were a child from a poor family at the beginning of Victorian times, you worked and worked and worked…

▲ ① Some children were used underground in the mines to push and pull trucks full of coal. The small size of children made it easier for them to fit into the small tunnels.

The city was becoming more prosperous. This new prosperity depended on the **MASS-PRODUCTION** of cheap goods in factories. The cheapness of such goods depended in turn on machines and on paying workers low wages. Not only were wages very low, but the work was hard and hours extremely long. Holidays were unknown.

The role of children

A factory might have been filled with machines, but the machines were not complex and automatic like the ones we are used to today. Early-Victorian machines needed constant attention. This is why a factory employed so many people – children as well as adults.

Adults were paid low wages. But children could be paid even less than adults. On such low pay, parents could not earn enough money to keep the family on their own. They needed even the pitiful amounts of money that their children could earn. So having children at work was not only vital to the factory owner but also to the poor working families.

Many children ate poor food, worked long hours and lived in damp, filthy conditions. As a result, many children died of disease. Those that survived looked like little old people.

▶ ② Children carry clay in a Victorian brickyard.

◀ ③ Other children were employed above ground, helping to move coal, iron, copper or other ores from the pithead to the railway.

What children did

You may wonder what use any children could be (pictures ①, ② and ③) – especially those as young as three or four.

One important reason was that children are small, and so can get to places adults cannot. In cotton mills, for example, they were regularly sent in amongst the machines to rethread them or do other tasks – usually while the machines were still running (see picture ④).

And in coal mines, children were used to pull trucks along tunnels too narrow for adults to fit into. Children were also used to do the jobs that no one else could be bothered to do.

For example, they were set to work picking up scraps from the factory floor or stoking the fires of the boilers of the steam engines that powered the machines.

Whatever they did, after a twelve-hour day, children were exhausted. If they were unlucky, they might have been injured or burned, too.

Many children were employed in new factories, looking after the machines. These machines had no safety guards on them, so they were very dangerous.

▲▶ ④ In early Victorian times, the youngest and smallest children were employed collecting waste that fell from the machines. They had to scamper about under the machines while the machines were still working.

Why didn't children refuse to work?

You may think that you would have refused to do such hard, dangerous work. But most children had no choice – they needed to work to help support their families and almost all the jobs on offer were hard.

What's more, most children could not ask for better wages because there were always plenty of jobless children who would take their place. If you wanted enough to eat, you had to take whatever job was on offer. This allowed children to be EXPLOITED by the factory owners.

Jobs for workhouse children

Each PARISH had a WORKHOUSE, in which the poorest people were put to work in exchange for giving them food and a place to sleep.

Because the parish had to pay for the workhouse, the parish wanted to get rid of its inmates as soon as possible. So one of the jobs of the workhouse manager – the beadle – was to seek jobs for the inmates. The jobs the beadle found were usually close to slavery.

Here is an example found in a letter written by the Vicar of Biddulph, in Staffordshire, to Samuel Greg, the owner of a textile factory:

"The thought has occurred to me that some of the younger branches {that is, the children} of the poor of this parish might be useful to you as apprentices in your factory at Quarry Bank, Styal, Cheshire. If you are in want of any of the above, we could readily furnish you with ten or more at from 9 to 12 years of age of both sexes."

Some parishes paid businessmen like Greg between two and four pounds to take a child off their hands. In return, the children received their board, lodging and a very small salary.

Factory owners saw themselves as doing a service to society. Here is a description that suggests the factory provided better conditions than in the workhouse:

> "At…the great firm of Greg and Son…stands a handsome house, two storeys high, built for the accommodation of the female apprentices. They are well fed, clothed and educated. The apprentices have milk-porridge for breakfast, potatoes and bacon for dinner, and meat on Sundays."

▼ ⑤ **During Victorian times the government allowed cheap food to come from overseas. British farmers could sell their food only if they charged less. So they paid their workers pitiful wages and bought farm machines so they could sack many of their workers. Because farm workers lived in tied cottages, the worker not only lost his job, but his house as well. So the farm worker and his whole family might find themselves turned out, with nowhere to go.**

Children in the countryside

Things were, if anything, worse in the countryside. If you were a son or a daughter of a farmhand, you would be one of the poorest people in the country. Your father would get very low wages and even these were not regular. During planting and harvest, the whole family would be out in the fields working from dawn to dusk (picture ⑤). However, during the winter there was very little work to be had and families went short.

Tied housing

Farm workers lived in tiny cottages owned by the farmer. Workers could live there only while they were working for the farmer. These homes were called **TIED COTTAGES**.

The farmer worked out what he thought the cottage rent was worth, and he took this from the worker's wages. So in the end, farm workers hardly got any money at all.

How conditions improved

The change in the lives of ordinary children changed dramatically during Victorian times. For example, in 1837 nearly all children worked. By 1891, however, all children went to school.

▼ ① Here is what conditions were like at the start of Victorian times. A queue of children line up for the tiny wage the manager saw fit to give them.

So far in this book you have seen how harsh the living conditions could be for poor people at the start of Victorian times (pictures ①, ② and ③). But by the time the Victorian age was over, huge changes had occurred. Here is why such change came about.

Realising that life was too hard

What seems hard and cruel depends on the way people see things. For example, for thousands of years people had owned slaves and thought nothing wrong in it. At the start of Victorian times, there were still slaves in the United States!

▼ ② In early Victorian times, city streets like this one in London were overcrowded and dirty. As the decades passed, however, new laws attempted to make city life cleaner and healthier.

CHURCH LANE
BLOOMSBURY

"…the boys whispered to each other, and winked at Oliver; while his next neighbours nudged him. Child as he was, he was desperate with hunger, and reckless with misery. He rose from the table; and advancing to the master, basin and spoon in hand, said: somewhat alarmed at his own temerity: 'Please, sir, I want some more.'"

Charles Dickens, *Oliver Twist* (1836–37)

◄▼ ③ Oliver in the workhouse dares to ask for more gruel… For many this famous scene in Charles Dickens' novel *Oliver Twist* sums up the cruelty and harsh conditions of early Victorian times.

So, although, *we* see the conditions during early Victorian times as harsh compared to what we are used to today, most factory owners of the time did not. To them, it was simply how the world worked.

Change happens when people begin to see that what is going on needs improving. For example, Robert Owen, who owned a textile mill in New Lanark near Glasgow (pictures ④ and ⑤), believed that children who got better food and worked shorter hours would do at least as much work. He set out to prove this in his own factory.

▲ ④ Robert Owen's New Lanark mills provided workers with far better conditions than were common for the time.

▶ ⑤ In 1816, Robert Owen was called before a committee in the House of Commons to answer questions about child labour in factories. Here are some of his responses.

Question: "At what age do you take children into your mills?"

Robert Owen: "At ten and upwards."

Question: "Why do you not employ children at an earlier age?"

Robert Owen: "Because I consider it to be injurious [harmful] to the children, and not beneficial to the proprietors [owners]."

Question: "Do you give instruction to any part of your population?"

Robert Owen: "Yes. To the children from three years old upwards, and to every other part of the population that choose to receive it."

Question: "If you do not employ children under ten, what would you do with them?"

Robert Owen: "Instruct them, and give them exercise."

Owen travelled the country trying to convince other mill owners that they would not lose money by improving conditions. But he alone was not able to bring about change. Writers and artists, too, played an important role in stirring up public opinion.

In 1839, for example, Frances Trollope wrote a novel about the life of young factory workers. It was called *Michael Armstrong: Factory Boy* and highlighted the appalling conditions in factories. Charles Dickens was doing the same in some of his novels.

There were also people who worked at improving the lot of the poor directly. One of the best known of these was Dr Thomas John Barnardo, who built homes for orphan children who would otherwise have slept rough. In these homes they slept upstairs and on the ground floor were given food and helped to learn a trade.

But in the end it was up to the politicians to make real and lasting changes.

Changing attitudes

Because of the growing public outcry about child labour, the government eventually set up a **COMMISSION** to investigate the issue. As part of its work, it asked children what their work was like. Here is the reply of one child who worked in a textile factory:

"I have frequently worked at the frame till I could scarcely get home, and in this state have been stopped by people in the streets who noticed me shuffling along, and advised me to work no more in the factories; but I was not my own master. During the day, I frequently counted the clock, and calculated how many hours I had still to remain at work; my evenings were spent in preparing for the following day – in rubbing my knees, ankles, elbows, and wrists with oil, etc. I went to bed, to cry myself to sleep, and pray that the Lord would take me to himself before morning."

Most factory owners didn't believe that conditions were as bad as the children said until they went back to their own factories and looked at their workers' conditions. For example, one factory owner wrote:

"At a meeting in Manchester a man claimed that a child in one mill walked twenty-four miles a day. I was surprised by this statement, therefore, when I went home, I went into my own factory, and with a clock before me, I watched a child at work, and having watched her for some time, I then calculated the distance she had to go in a day, and to my surprise, I found it nothing short of twenty miles."

New laws

The first government law – called an **ACT OF PARLIAMENT** – was introduced in 1833, after a campaign in Parliament by Lord Ashley, later the Earl of Shaftesbury. It said:

"...no person under the age of eighteen years shall be employed in any such mill or factory more than twelve hours in any one day, nor more than sixty-nine hours in any one week... And be it further enacted that there shall be allowed in the course of every day not less than one and a half hours for meals to every such person... [people today work something like 35 hours a week]"

However, the Act only applied to children working in textile mills. So, throughout Victorian times, more Acts of Parliament were needed to improve conditions for children working in mines and elsewhere.

In 1842 the Mines Act made it illegal for children under ten to be employed underground in mines, and in 1844 the Factory Act made it illegal to employ children between eight and thirteen years for more than six and a half hours per day.

However, it took until 1847 for the working day for women and children in textile factories to be reduced to ten hours and it took until the 1870s before these better conditions applied to anywhere other than the mills.

In 1870, the Education Act set up schools for all children for the first time, taking young children away from factories for ever (see pages 26–27).

Why did children become healthier?

During Victorian times, people's chances of living to old age improved greatly.

As we have seen, life was tough for most people in Victorian times. But despite this, fewer children died and so the population grew quickly. Never in the whole of human history had this happened before. So what stopped so many children dying? The reason, to a large extent, was that they had become healthier.

Calling for change

There were three groups of people who were important in making Victorian children healthier.

❶ Doctors, nurses and scientists who discovered how to prevent disease.

❷ The politicians and newspapers who campaigned for shorter working hours and better working conditions.

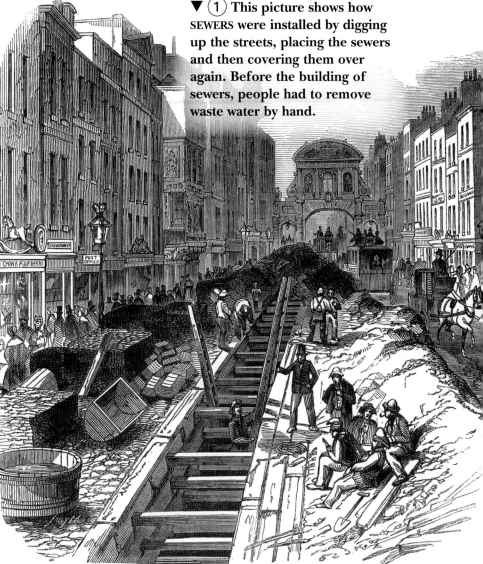

▼ ① This picture shows how SEWERS were installed by digging up the streets, placing the sewers and then covering them over again. Before the building of sewers, people had to remove waste water by hand.

❸ The engineers who cleaned up the water people drank.
One group could not have been successful without the other – all were needed.

Doctors and nurses

During Victorian times, there was a great increase in the understanding of disease. People like the hospital surgeon Dr Joseph Lister and

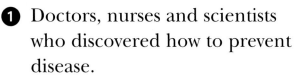

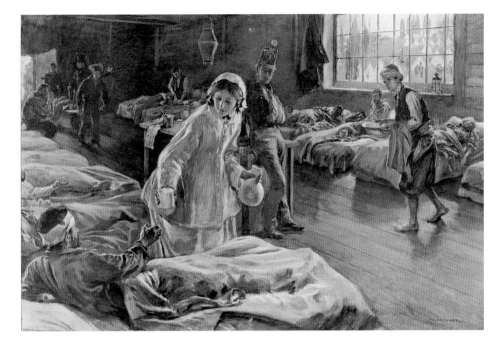

◀ ② Florence Nightingale was important for her pioneering work in reducing infection in hospitals.

▼ ③ This is the map that Dr John Snow used to plot the cases of cholera in the City of London. He saw that they were all concentrated around a single water pump. When he removed the handle of the pump and people could no longer use the polluted water, the disease stopped. It was a clear sign that polluted water was the cause of disease.

nurse Florence Nightingale (picture ②) understood that disease could be reduced by cleanliness and by using chemicals called **ANTISEPTICS**.

Others, like Dr John Snow kept records of illnesses and found patterns that helped to understand how diseases like **CHOLERA** were spread in polluted water (picture ③). In France, meanwhile, Louis Pasteur made the first **VACCINES** to ward off disease.

Clean water

In early Victorian times, people thought that diseases were passed from person to person through the smells in the air. So they worried about how they could keep the stench of pollution away.

One way they did this was to build great water systems in cities,

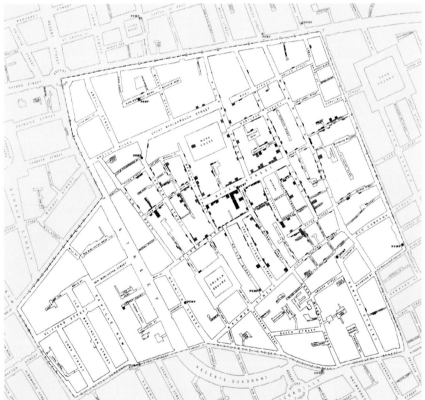

to pipe cleaned water to taps and to pipe the dirty water away (picture ①). The clean water removed the stench – and also the bacteria in the water that caused so much disease.

Class

People in Victorian times were very concerned about their 'class' – that is, their position in society. Mixing with people – let alone marrying someone – from a lower class was frowned upon. Even in church there were different pews for different classes.

Victorian society was strictly divided up into three classes – upper class, middle class and lower, or working, class. Belonging to a certain class meant that you were expected to behave and dress in a certain way.

Children belonged to the same class as their parents and, as they grew up, they quickly learned how they were expected to behave.

Sometimes people who became richer – through trade, for example – were able to 'better themselves' – that is, join a higher social class.

Upper class

Top hat

Moustaches and sideburns

Straw hat called a **BOATER**

'Tam-o'-shanter' woollen beret

▼ ① Upper- and middle-class dress

Narrow waist held in with **CORSETS**.

Flared skirt, or **BUSTLE**

Kilts for boys

Boots

Another way to change class was through marriage, although this was often disapproved of.

Being upper class

To be upper class you had to be related to royalty or the nobility in some way. As a member of the upper classes, you probably owned large amounts of land and large houses, both in the countryside and in London. You might have a title such as Lord, Sir or Lady.

Being middle class

To be middle class, your father usually worked in one of the 'professions' – he might be a lawyer, a vicar, a doctor, or

Waistcoat

Frock coat

Middle class

Snood (bag-like net)

The Victorians lived by sets of rules. These governed what they did, how they dressed, and how they entertained. They also governed how people spoke to one another.

Here are some examples of rules followed by middle-class Victorians:

❶ Never point or stare at someone.
❷ Never ask about the private matters of others.
❸ Speak in a calm manner using respectful language.
❹ Do not always start a conversation with the weather.
❺ Do not brag about your 'birth' or your acquaintance with distinguished or wealthy people.
❻ Do not speak of religion or politics or gossip.
❼ Children should be seen but not heard.
❽ The hostess must sit opposite her husband in a dinner party.
❾ Guests should arrive within 15 minutes of the appointed time.
❿ Do not open your mouth while chewing or make noises with your throat.
⓫ Use a napkin to clean your fingers.
⓬ Do not wave your cutlery around in order to make a point of conversation.
⓭ Never discuss at the table why certain foods do not agree with you.

an officer in the army, for example. These positions commanded respect from the community.

Even within the middle class, there were different levels according to how much money you had or how important your job was.

If you were *upper* middle class, you might live in a big detached house (a villa) with several servants, including a **GOVERNESS** to look after and teach the children.

If you were *lower* middle class, you might live in what you called a 'villa' in the suburbs. These villas were often in terraces like working-class houses, but they were bigger. There was usually room for one live-in servant who lived in the attic (see page 43, picture ③).

If your father was near the bottom of the middle classes, he might find servants too expensive. So, to make sure people knew his family was still middle class, he would insist on being called 'Mr' at work rather than just by his last name.

Middle class women did not work. Women were expected to stay at home to manage the household and look after the children. They had very few opportunities outside the home.

Upper- and middle-class children's clothes

Dress was an important part of showing to which class you belonged. But, of course, only middle- and upper-class families had the money to dress fashionably (picture ①, pages 18–19).

Throughout the century small children – both boys and girls! – wore frocks and white frilly lace trousers under their frocks. Small boys wore their hair long, often with lots of curls. When they reached about six years old, however, boys began to wear tunics and

▼ ② **Lower-class dress**

Flat cap

Jacket

Scarf

Shawl

Top hat

Moleskin trousers

Wooden clogs

Hobnail boots

Apron

Clogs

Children dressed the same as adults

Working-class people were often much smaller than people from other classes. This was due to poor food.

Hand-me-down clothes were often too big

Woollen clothes

Mended or patched clothes

Pinafore

Being lower class

If your father worked with his hands, he belonged to the lower classes. If your father was at the top of the lower class (and had a chance of becoming middle class), he would have been a tradesman (a butcher, for example) or a craftsman (such as a carpenter). You would probably live in a small terraced house.

If your father was not that skilled (such as a plumber's mate), then he came below the skilled people.

If your father was unskilled (such as a street cleaner) but in regular work, he was next down the scale. Your family would probably rent a room or two in someone else's house. People without regular work were at the bottom of the lower classes.

Lower-class children's clothes

The lower classes wore completely different clothes (picture ②) because they had to do manual work for a living. They had to have hard-wearing clothes, and they could not afford to follow fashion. Boys were dressed in shirt and trousers as soon as possible. Even young boys wore a flat cap. They also wore heavy, hard-wearing leather boots or wooden clogs.

Most small children were dressed in ill-fitting clothes because they simply wore what were handed down from older children or even adults. As a result, young children often looked like little men and women.

suits. This stage in a boyhood was known as 'breeching' – the Victorian word for trousers was breeches.

Queen Victoria often dressed her own sons in kilts and sailor suits (see pages 22–23, picture ①), and the upper and middle classes quickly copied her example. Others dressed their sons in a velvet suit known as a 'Little Lord Fauntleroy', after a character in a popular children's book. Girls wore pinafores.

Games, toys and pastimes

Upper- and middle-class children enjoyed many sports and pastimes. Poor children had few or no toys and few chances to play with them.

By the end of Victorian times, many people were working shorter hours and had more money to spend on their children.

City and town authorities built parks, museums and libraries for citizens to enjoy. Children never went to these places alone but in the company of adults – their parents or a **GOVERNESS**.

Toys and games

At home, the younger children of wealthy families might have a nursery – a room where they could play and learn (picture ①). They played with wooden toys or sang nursery rhymes. Working-class children had no toys; they were often too busy working.

Rocking-horse

'Little Lord Fauntleroy' suit

Noah's Ark

▼ ① **A typical upper-middle-class Victorian nursery. Outside, children play with hoops, while inside the children play with toys such as hobby horses and doll's houses. Notice the children's clothes, too.**

Hoops

Doll's-house

Hobby-horse

Spinning top

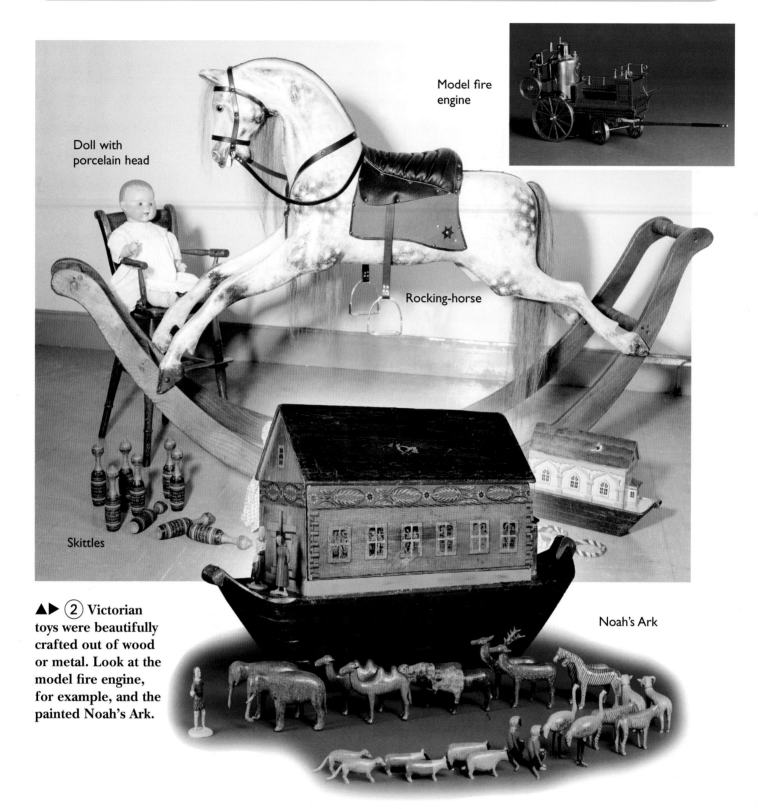

Model fire engine

Doll with porcelain head

Rocking-horse

Skittles

Noah's Ark

▲▶ ② Victorian toys were beautifully crafted out of wood or metal. Look at the model fire engine, for example, and the painted Noah's Ark.

In later Victorian times toys began to be made in factories, making them cheaper to buy. There was soon a huge variety of factory-made toys to be bought. Top of the list for all young middle-class children was the wooden rocking-horse (picture ②). Girls had dolls (pictures ② and ③) and doll's-houses. Boys had tin soldiers, clockwork train sets, spinning tops and marbles. Most children also played with hoops.

Older middle-class children might play with toy theatres. They would also read and play board games. However, they never used dice as this was considered 'gambling'. Older girls might also sew.

Some children kept scrapbooks (meaning 'scraps' of information). Into these, they pasted pictures of their favourite things and people, together with short descriptions or lines of poetry.

Sports

Both Victorian children and adults enjoyed sport, which they considered – quite rightly – good for their health. The Victorians believed in 'fair play' and developed proper sets of rules for football, cricket and boxing.

Working-class men particularly liked football. Teams were set up by local churches or factories, and whole communities turned out to watch their local team play.

Croquet and lawn tennis were played first by middle-class women and later on by men. Cycling was also a very popular middle-class pastime after the invention of the **SAFETY BICYCLE** in 1885. It was cheap, healthy and could get you out into the countryside.

Music and entertainment

A popular family pastime in middle- and upper-class households was playing the piano and singing. Lower-class men might play in a local brass band or sing in a choir. Many lower-class people enjoyed going to the **MUSIC HALL**.

◄ ③ An upper-middle-class Victorian family on an 'outing'. The two smallest children have dolls.

Weblink: www.CurriculumVisions.com

Going to school

Education was made compulsory after 1870 and free after 1891, but learning was very different from what it is now.

> *"Now, what I want is, Facts. Teach these boys and girls nothing but Facts. Facts alone are wanted in life. Plant nothing else, and root out everything else!"*
>
> **Charles Dickens, *Hard Times* (1854)**

Few children went to school in early Victorian times. Some went to Sunday schools, which were run by churches. Upper-class and some middle-class children were taught by a **GOVERNESS** at home. Everything changed with the Education Act of 1870, which made school compulsory for children aged five to ten. Learning in Victorian schools was very different from what it is today. Today when you are asked a question you are expected to work out an answer in your head. In a Victorian schoolroom, by contrast, you were expected to recite the answer you had been taught.

Punishment

Most Victorian children did not ask questions, but simply learned facts told them by the teacher. Whenever a teacher spoke to a pupil, the pupil first stood up and only then answered the question.

If they got a question wrong they might be placed in the corner of the room with a dunce's cap on. If they spoke without being asked they might be struck with a ruler and if naughty or late at school they were likely to be beaten with a cane.

'The Three Rs'

All children learned at least the 'three Rs': reading, writing and arithmetic. This may seem very straightforward, but you have to remember that before this time most children would not have been able to read or write. So doing these simple things was a great achievement. The Victorians believed that these skills were an important way people could improve themselves. Arithmetic, for example, was important in most trades and so was the key to a better-paid job.

Some parents thought schooling was a waste of time. When children were at school they were not available to work, so some parents kept them away 'sick'.

A city schoolroom

In a city like London or Liverpool, schools might have as many as twenty classrooms. There might be forty children in each class, and they were taught all subjects by a single teacher.

▲ ① **Victorian classrooms were very crowded. On the walls were maps of the Empire and pictures of the Royal Family and of other famous Victorians. Notice also the gas lighting.**

School materials were expensive. Younger children wrote using a slate (made from stone) and chalk. They rubbed the chalk out with their cuffs. As they got older, children learned to write with a pen and ink on paper in a **COPYBOOK**.

Most schoolrooms had desks rather than tables. Pupils sat in rows on benches behind the desks (picture ①). Often older children helped younger children with their lessons, acting as unpaid classroom assistants.

The school day

Each day began with the teacher saying 'Good morning, class' and the class would say 'Good morning, sir,' or 'Good morning, ma'am'. The teacher would read out and mark the register. He or she would also check that everyone was dressed properly.

Next came prayers, followed by a lesson in arithmetic. The next class might be geography, which included reciting the names of capital cities and the countries that belonged to the British Empire.

A spelling lesson might involve the teacher 'dictating' a difficult poem for the children to write or getting them to copy out sentences from the blackboard. The school day ended only at 5 p.m. – although usually children did go home for lunch.

The railway arrives!

The railway was the single most important thing that changed the way Victorians lived.

The coming of the railways transformed Britain (picture ①). Railways changed a journey of weeks into hours; they helped create the **SUBURBS** of our cities, and they even made it possible for people to have holidays at the seaside.

Before the railways

For thousands of years, people had travelled on foot, by horse or by boat. Whichever of these means of transport they chose, it was slow. It was also impossible to carry large amounts of goods. As a result, goods were expensive.

Change started with the Industrial Revolution in the late 18th century, when factories began to mass-produce cheap goods. Canals were built around the country to carry these goods from the factories to the cities, where they were sold. But barges were drawn by horses and so goods still moved slowly.

Railways could carry goods many times faster than barges, and track could be laid far more cheaply than canals could be dug. So railways allowed more goods to be delivered cheaply to more people.

▼ ① This early-19th-century drawing shows the different uses to which the railway was put: Passengers could travel quickly around the country while manufactured goods or livestock could be transported to where they were needed.

The railways were also responsible for changes at the seaside. You will find more about this on page 32.

HOW DID LIFE CHANGE IN VICTORIAN TIMES?

Railway mania

The first goods railway ran between Stockton and Darlington in 1825. The first passenger train ran a year later between Liverpool and Manchester.

But the railway age really got under way in Victorian times. In the 1840s, there were tracks being laid, bridges being built and tunnels being dug all over the country (picture ②).

Making room for a railway

Railways needed to come into the heart of towns and cities. But railway lines and stations take up a lot of space. Some people were bound to benefit, while others might suffer. So who was for and against the railway?

The table below shows you that it was a surprisingly even debate. But in the end, those in favour won the day and 'railway mania' set in.

For the railway

► Factory owners, who knew that goods could reach more places more speedily with the railways than by using canals. So they would sell more goods.

► The mayor and council, who saw the railway as bringing jobs and prosperity for their town or city.

► Workers, who saw it as a chance to find a job.

► Landowners, who saw a chance to sell land at a good profit.

► People who felt it was a new and exciting way of life. People were fascinated by the chance to be pulled along by a machine instead of a horse. "You skim along like magic," one Victorian enthusiast declared.

Against the railway

► Some country landowners, because they thought the railway would ruin their lands.

► The people who lived along the route of the railway, because they would lose their homes. In a city, large numbers of houses had to be demolished to make way for tracks and a station.

► Canal and barge owners, stagecoach owners and innkeepers, who were all alarmed because they could see their way of life disappearing.

► Those who thought the railways would divide up the city, making it impossible to get from one area to another because they were separated by the tracks.

► People who worried about what effect the speed of the trains might have on the human body!

▲ ② Sometimes the railway developers built massive railway bridges, or viaducts, which arched over the city houses below. Many other houses, however, were simply demolished.

Railways cause cities to spread

In the early years, a ticket on a train was hugely expensive and only the middle and upper classes could afford to travel this way. The railway companies needed to find a way to get more people to travel.

Remember that, in Victorian times, the numbers of people in the cities was growing quickly and getting more and more crowded.

In the 1870s, the railway companies began to build stations on the edge of the towns and cities. They also featured a 'workman's ticket', which was far cheaper than the normal ticket price. So now people could afford to live further from their factories and offices.

Builders quickly created little villages of shops and homes around these new stations. The middle classes were the first to move, buying villas (see pages 20, 34–35 and 43) in what were then country lanes by the station. Working-class housing followed later.

The Victorian suburbs have since been surrounded by modern suburbs, and what the Victorians called suburbs are now part of the modern inner city.

Victorians invent the seaside

Most seaside towns grew up in Victorian times, thanks to the railways and the invention of holidays.

PADDLING AT BRIGHTON.

The railway was not just responsible for changing the face of the towns and cities. It was also responsible for changing the seaside.

At the start of Victorian times, most people would never have been to the seaside. The only means of travelling was by horse and carriage and the only buildings were fishermen's cottages and homes for the wealthy.

The railways made it possible for people to reach the seaside more cheaply and easily. Places that had before seemed remote, such as St Ives in Cornwall or Blackpool in Lancashire, now became accessible.

Bank holidays

During middle Victorian times, more and more middle-class people got paid holiday time and some chose to buy villas by the sea. Many buildings now used as guest houses began as

▲ ① **This Victorian postcard shows a group of women and children paddling. Victorian people wore very different clothes on the beach to what we are used to today. Bathing clothes covered as much of the body as possible – partly because it was considered immodest to show too much flesh and partly because sun-tanned skin was thought to be 'lower-class'.**

homes of this kind. Others went to stay in the new grand hotels.

Then, in 1871, the government introduced the first official public holidays. Now even the lower classes had time for a day trip to the seaside. The railway companies responded by providing fourth-class carriages for working people to travel in.

The changing seaside

Many seaside towns now changed completely. The working-class day-trippers had different needs to the middle classes in their villas. The lower classes wanted entertainment. As a result, attractions such as **MUSIC HALLS** and funfairs were built for them.

For all these reasons, going for a holiday to the seaside became an important part of the Victorian way of life.

What the seaside was like

The Victorians did not use the seaside as we do today (pictures ① and ②). For example, nobody sunbathed. Instead, people walked along the **PROMENADE** or along the **PIER**, and enjoyed entertainments such as music played by an organ-grinder or a Punch and Judy puppet show.

Public bathing was not allowed. If people went swimming, they used private bathing machines which were wheeled into the sea.

Which seaside places were most popular?

For those in the north, there were nearby Blackpool in Lancashire and Scarborough in Yorkshire. Those in the Midlands travelled to Weston-super-Mare in Somerset and Skegness in Lincolnshire. Those in London went down the Thames to Southend-on-Sea or to Broadstairs and Brighton. Those in Glasgow went mainly to Helensburgh.

Jobs at the seaside

There was an army of people employed in seaside towns. They cleaned, fetched and carried, or ran **PUBLIC HOUSES**, hotels, funfairs, dance halls and so on. The seaside had become big business.

▼ ② Many middle class Victorians spent their seaside holidays strolling along the seafront on a special path called a promenade. Notice the grand new hotels that line the seafront and the bathing machines at the top of the beach.

What home was like

Some families were wealthy enough to have servants, while other families crowded into a single rented room.

The home you live in depends on how much money you can afford to pay. In Victorian times, lower-class housing was very different from middle-class housing.

The middle-class villa

By the middle of Victorian times, the upper middle classes could afford larger houses. People such as doctors and lawyers, factory managers and shopowners were becoming very wealthy. They had large families and could afford servants.

Their houses therefore had to be large, too (pictures ① and ②).

After a day's outing, the family arrived home by carriage. As they climbed the flight of steps up to their front door, their carriage and horses were taken round the back to the stables in the MEWS.

While the parents took tea in the drawing room, the children went to their nursery and their governess. Meanwhile, in the basement, the cook was busy preparing food.

▼ ① These typical London town houses were built as homes for the Victorian upper middle classes. The houses were built on wide leafy streets and included several storeys.

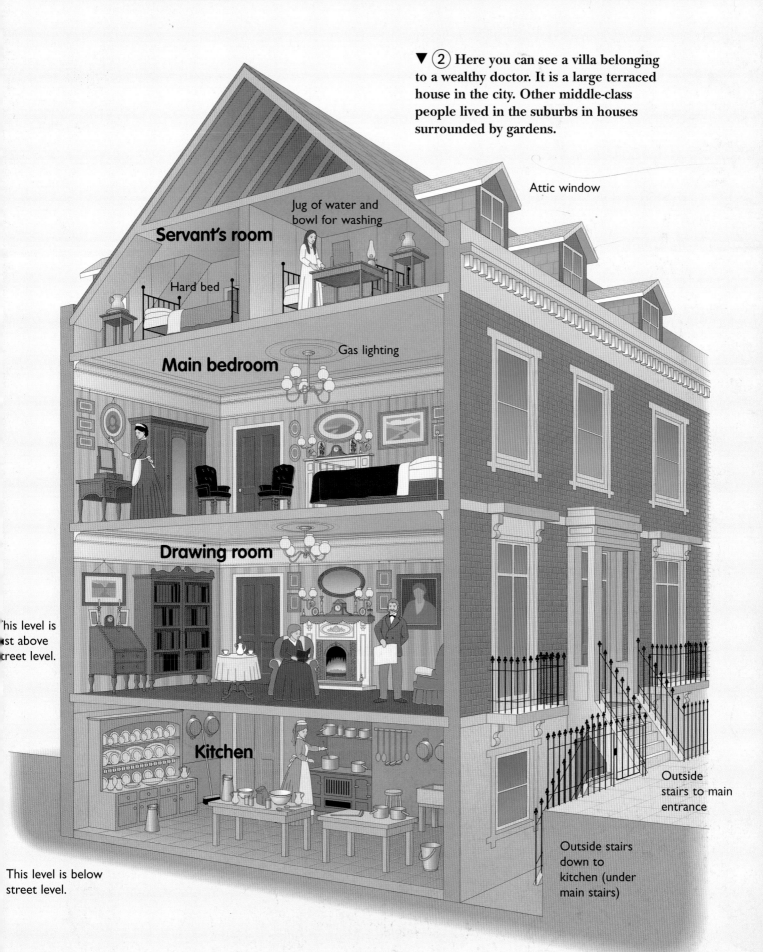

▼ ② Here you can see a villa belonging to a wealthy doctor. It is a large terraced house in the city. Other middle-class people lived in the suburbs in houses surrounded by gardens.

Attic window

Servant's room

Jug of water and bowl for washing

Hard bed

Main bedroom

Gas lighting

Drawing room

This level is just above street level.

Kitchen

Outside stairs to main entrance

Outside stairs down to kitchen (under main stairs)

This level is below street level.

Above the living rooms were the bedrooms. The spacious ones on the first floor were for the family, and the smaller ones above were for the servants.

The lower-class terraced house

Most people in the lower classes could not afford to buy their homes and had to rent. They were rented by landlords who were often lower class, too. Some people rented apartments above shops. Others rented small terraced houses, or even just one or two rooms in a terraced house (pictures ③ and ④).

At the bottom end of the housing scale were the crowded, badly built apartment blocks called **TENEMENTS**.

Three-quarters of all people living in Victorian British cities lived in one of these overcrowded buildings. Each family might have just one room or, if they were lucky, two rooms in the tenement.

There was no running water. Instead, water had to be fetched from a pump in the street. An outside toilet, called a privvy, was shared by a large number of neighbours (see page 5, picture ②).

There was no gas or electricity. Instead rooms were lit with an oil lamp.

But although conditions were grim, it did not mean that people took no pride in their homes. Often the reverse was true and people kept their tiny houses neat and clean at a time when chimney smoke made everything filthy within hours.

▼ ③ A lower-class street of terraced housing with a group of shops near the end of the row.

QUEBEC ST. LANGLEY PARK

▼ ④ Here you can see working-class terrace houses of later Victorian times. By this time, working-class housing was improving. The rooms are small but kept clean and tidy. This house has a toilet in a small extension – after 1874 all new houses had to have their own toilet.

Attic

Bedroom

Parlour

Toilet

Coal cellar

Cellar

37

Victorians go shopping

The Victorians invented shopping as we know today...

For hundreds of years, most people had little money and bought things rarely. They mostly grew their own food. If you wanted something, you had it made for you. There were no machines to mass-produce things cheaply, so anything you bought was expensive. If you were wealthy, the makers came to you. So there was no need for shops.

Shops

In Victorian times, all of this turned on its head. People had more money. They lived in cities and so could not produce their own food. Machines in factories made a wide range of goods cheaply. So the people who made things needed to find a convenient way of selling their goods to the people who wanted them. This is how the shop came to be invented.

▲▶ ① Inside (above) and outside (opposite) a general store.

Different kinds of shop

The Victorians developed three quite different types of shop. You can still find them all today.

For food and everyday items they invented the corner shop, or general store (picture ①). Their customers lived in the nearby streets. For things that were needed less often (for example dresses or shoes) they invented the high street shop. For the wealthy, they developed the department store where a great range of luxury goods were on sale.

1891 – Late Victorian times

Towards the end of Victorian times, there were schools for all, clean water, cheap railways and even holidays. Life was still tough for the poor, but much better than at the start of Victorian times.

There had been enormous changes since Queen Victoria came to the throne in 1837.

For one thing, the 1891 CENSUS showed that there were nearly twice as many people as at the start of Victorian times. Far more children lived to be adults and far more adults lived into old age.

People are better off

The cities had not been swamped by all these people. Nor had life got worse. In fact, quite the reverse was true. Between 1860 and the end of Victorian times, real wages almost doubled while prices fell by half. As a result, for many people, especially the middle classes, it was a time of prosperity – they had the money to buy things that had never been possible before.

Planning

In previous centuries towns and cities had grown chaotically. Now councils began to plan where houses and shops should go (picture ①). They built schools and hospitals and laid out city parks. The city councils became so powerful that they built themselves

grand offices – city and town halls. They also began to employ more and more people.

▼ ① A view of a city about 1891 as seen on a rainy day. Compare it with the city of 1837 shown on pages 6 to 7.

Factories

Water-treatment plant

Hospital

School

Terraced homes with toilets

Tram

Street lighting

Rows of terraced working-class housing. The extensions at the back are toilets.

HOW DID LIFE CHANGE IN VICTORIAN TIMES?

Railways and **TRAMS** had made it easier for people to travel, and cities began to spread out. The **SUBURBS** were invented. At the same time, the number of **SLUMS** began to fall.

Clean water arrived in most houses, and flush toilets, too. City councils collected rubbish and built public baths for those without baths at home. They even installed street lights.

In many ways, the Victorians laid down the foundations for life as we know it today. For this reason, many people look back to Victorian times as one of the greatest times in British history. Without the Victorians, we would lack many of the things we take for granted today – from the museums and public libraries we visit to the railways we travel on!

Prison

City hall

To railway suburbs

Railway station

Railway

Music hall

Canal

Workhouse

Shopping street

Paved roads

Park

Shopping street

Slums remain in 'courts' behind main roads

Sewers built under roads

River

What the Victorians left for us

The Victorian age ended just over a century ago. But many Victorian buildings – from houses to parks and museums – are still all around us. Here is how to identify Victorian buildings.

The Victorians were good builders and, in any case, because Victorian times only ended a century ago, much of what they built has survived. Some of it has been left untouched, but much has been altered (picture ①).

Does my area have any Victorian buildings?

You will find Victorian buildings in these kinds of places:
▶ by docks and railway stations
▶ in most seaside towns
▶ in town/city centres
▶ in the more densely packed inner parts of cities
▶ in country villages

'Heavy' stone decoration to windows

PRINCIPLES

BT

The ground floor has been redesigned for modern use.

▲ ① When you are looking for traces of Victorian shops, look *up*. Ground floors have often been redesigned for modern use, but the upper floors often look much as they did in Victorian times.

You will rarely find Victorian buildings in these places:
▶ New-Towns, unless the town grew from something much older
▶ the 'outer suburbs' of cities – this is because these were built after Victorian times

What kinds of buildings are there?

Many surviving Victorian buildings are those intended for public use, such as town halls (picture ②), schools, libraries, museums, railway stations,

▲ ② **The Victorians built many beautiful and lavish town halls. This shows how important and powerful town councils had become by this time. Leeds Town Hall, shown here, was opened by Queen Victoria in 1858.**

police stations and hospitals. Terraced housing (picture ③), too, is likely to date from Victorian times.

Dating buildings

There are lots of clues that can help you spot a Victorian building. Many public buildings from the time included a date on the facade, or front.

On a school, look for the doors that have 'Boys' and 'Girls' marked over them. Victorian houses often had names written over the front door – for example, Amelia Villas.

In terraced houses, look at the ground-floor windows. If they are flat-fronted, they probably belonged to lower-class Victorians. If they are bay-fronted, they were inhabited by the middle classes.

Victorians liked to decorate their houses with tiles and coloured bricks. The window frames are 'heavy'-looking, and on bay windows they are often made from stone.

Victorian homes didn't, of course, have garages. But large houses often had stables, which were reached by back alleys called MEWS.

Finally, you may be able to tell a Victorian part of a city by a gridiron (criss-cross) road plan. This was rarely used in later times.

◄ ③ **A terrace (continuous row) of middle-class houses with bay-front windows. The room in the roof would have been where a servant once lived.**

Weblink: www.CurriculumVisions.com

Some famous Victorians

Some important people of Victorian times.

ANDERSON, ELIZABETH GARRETT (1836–1917)
The first woman to qualify as a doctor in Britain. She founded a hospital for poor women and children in London.

ASHLEY, LORD (EARL OF SHAFTESBURY) (1801–1885)
An important Victorian social reformer. As a Member of Parliament, he drafted many of the laws that improved the working conditions of ordinary people. One such law was the Mines Act of 1847, which banned women and children under ten from working underground.

BARNARDO, DR THOMAS JOHN (1845–1905)
Born in Ireland, Barnardo came to London in 1866. He founded more than 90 homes for homeless children, the first of which opened in 1870.

BEETON, ISABELLA (1836–1865)
An English writer whose *Book of Household Management* was a best-seller for many years.

BELL, ALEXANDER GRAHAM (1847–1922)
Inventor of the telephone.

BOOTH, WILLIAM (1829–1912)
A Methodist minister who founded the Salvation Army in 1878 to preach and give help, shelter and food to poor people.

BRUNEL, ISAMBARD KINGDOM (1806–1859)
Brunel was an engineer who specialised in railway traction, tunnels, steamships and bridges. He designed the Clifton Suspension Bridge and was engineer to the Great Western Railway. He built the SS *Great Eastern*, the largest 19th-century ship. He also built the first ship made with a metal hull.

CADBURY'S
John Cadbury was one of ten children born into a Quaker family in Birmingham. He opened his first shop in 1824. He sold tea and coffee as well as drinking chocolate, which he prepared himself using a mortar and pestle. The products were sold in blocks: customers then scraped a little off into a cup or saucepan and added hot milk or water.

The business developed and was taken over by John Cadbury's sons, who started up a new factory in Bournville to provide better working and living conditions for their employees. The name 'Bournville' was made up from 'Bourn' from the nearby stream and 'ville', the French word for town. Bournville became one of a number of model villages for working people in Victorian times.

CARROLL, LEWIS (1832–1898)
The author of *Alice in Wonderland* (1865). His real name was Charles L. Dodgson.

DARWIN, CHARLES (1809–1882)
An English naturalist who was famous for his theory of 'natural selection'. As a young scientist he accompanied an expedition on a ship named the *Beagle* and came back with observations on the varieties of fossils and living animals. He published his findings in *The Origin of Species* in 1859. Because he questioned the story of creation found in the Bible, his ideas caused outrage and fierce debate.

DICKENS, CHARLES (1812–1870)
Great novelist of the Victorian age. His novels were extremely popular in his time and today they are 'classics'. His books include stories about thieves, convicts and schoolboys. He wrote about ordinary people and how they lived, about terrible prisons, bad schools and the workhouse. His famous characters include Oliver Twist, Scrooge and David Copperfield.

DISRAELI, BENJAMIN (1804–1881)
A Victorian prime minister. An author as well as a politician, Disraeli wore fancy clothes and loved to make fun of his rival, Gladstone.

CONAN DOYLE, ARTHUR (1859–1930)
Writer who created the detective Sherlock Holmes.

EVANS, MARY ANN (1819–1880)
Author who wrote a number of books under the pen name 'George Eliot'. Her well-known books include *Mill on the Floss* and *Middlemarch*.

GLADSTONE, WILLIAM (1809–1898)
A Victorian politician who was prime minister four times. He was a very religious man who turned down a career in the church to become a politician. He had a strong sense of right and wrong and believed people should be judged on their merits, not on their wealth.

GRACE, W.G. (1848–1915)
An all-round cricketer who broke many cricketing records and made the game popular.

HARDY, THOMAS (1840–1928)
An English novelist and poet who was born in Dorset. He wrote many stories set in the fictitious county of Wessex. These included *Tess of the D'Urbervilles* and *The Mayor of Casterbridge*.

KELVIN, LORD WILLIAM THOMSON (1824–1907)
A Scottish mathematician and physicist. The scientific unit of temperature, the Kelvin (K), is named after him.

KINGSLEY, MARY (1862–1900)
At the age of 30, Kingsley made two adventurous trips to West Africa where she collected information about African tribal customs.

KIPLING, RUDYARD (1865–1936)

A Victorian writer born in Bombay, India, but educated in England. He became chiefly known as a writer of short stories. Kipling was an ardent supporter of the British Empire and wrote many collections of poems including *Plain Tales from the Hills* (1888) and *Soldiers Three* (1888). In 1894 his *Jungle Book* was published and became a children's classic all over the world. He also wrote *Kim* (1901).

LIPTON, SIR THOMAS J. (1850–1931)

Born in Glasgow, Lipton developed a chain of stores and was the first to standardise products. He began to offer high quality products at a fair price by buying teas directly from his suppliers. He acquired several tea estates and became his own supplier of tea. He promoted Lipton tea as 'direct from the gardens to the teapot'. He was a millionaire by the age of 30. Sir Thomas left much of his fortune to the city of Glasgow, to aid the poor and to build hospitals. Sir Thomas also introduced the tea bag.

LISTER, DR JOSEPH (LATER BARON LISTER) (1827–1912)

A pioneer of the use of antiseptics during surgery. Lister's main idea that bacteria must not enter a wound during an operation is still followed today.

LIVINGSTONE, DR DAVID (1813–1873)

A missionary who made three long explorations of East Africa. He wrote the story of his amazing three-year journey across Africa from the Atlantic to the Indian Ocean. He was the first European to see the waterfall the local people called 'the falls of a thousand smokes'. Livingstone gave it its English name, the Victoria Falls, after the British queen.

MARX, KARL (1818–1883)

Karl Marx was born in Germany. Marx was a thinker who helped develop the ideas of Communism. Marx was banished from Paris in 1845 as a dangerous revolutionary. He was then banished from Belgium in February 1848, and finally ended up in London in 1849 where he lived until his death. He is buried at Highgate Cemetery in London.

NIGHTINGALE, FLORENCE (1820–1910)

'The Lady with the Lamp' and the founder of modern nursing. In 1854, she took charge of nursing soldiers wounded in the Crimean War. She organised the cleaning of the military hospital and organised proper nursing. The death rate fell dramatically.

OWEN, ROBERT (1771–1858)

A Welsh-born manufacturer and reformer. He founded a model village at New Lanark in Scotland and later helped set up the model community of New Harmony in the United States. His ideas influenced many Victorian social reformers.

PARNELL, CHARLES STEWART (1846–1891)

An Irish political leader who became an MP in 1875 and argued passionately for Irish independence.

PEEL, ROBERT (1788–1850)

Prime minister who reformed many laws in late Georgian and early Victorian times.

POTTER, BEATRIX (1866–1943)

Beatrix Potter was born in London but her parents also rented a house in the Lake District. This is where she watched squirrels in the woods and saw rabbits in the vegetable gardens of the big house. She made many sketches of the landscape and wrote *The Tale of Peter Rabbit* in the last year of Victoria's reign. It was published in 1902.

SAINSBURY, JOHN AND MARY

Sainsbury's was founded in 1869 by John James and Mary Ann Sainsbury. They opened their first small dairy shop in Drury Lane, London. Drury Lane was one of London's poorest areas and the Sainsburys' shop quickly became popular for offering high-quality products at low prices. By 1882, John James Sainsbury had four shops and was producing the Sainsbury's first own-brand product – bacon. John James stepped up his rate of expansion so that he could buy goods as competitively as companies such as Liptons. Between 1890 and 1900, the number of Sainsbury's branches trebled from 16 to 48.

SNOW, DR JOHN (1813–1858)

A scientific whose researches into how diseases spread enabled the Victorians to improve the health of millions of people. In his book, *On the Mode of Communication of Cholera* (1849), he argued – rightly – that the disease was carried through dirty water.

STEVENSON, ROBERT LOUIS (1850–1894)

Scottish author who wrote *Treasure Island* and *Kidnapped*, which are two of the most popular children's stories ever written.

STOKER, BRAM (1847–1912)

Abraham 'Bram' Stoker was born in Clontarf, Ireland on 8 November, 1847. In 1878, Stoker moved to London and in 1897 published *Dracula*, the story of a vampire.

TENNYSON, ALFRED LORD (1809–1892)

One of the most famous Victorian poets. He wrote many poems about major events of the time. One of the most famous is 'The Charge of the Light Brigade' about an incident during the Crimean War.

TROLLOPE, FRANCES (1780–1863)

A famous Victorian novelist who wrote more than 40 books. She often tackled the big issues of the day in her work such as slavery and the employment of children in factories. Her son Anthony Trollope was also a very famous Victorian novelist.

VICTORIA, QUEEN (1819–1901)

Victoria was born in 1819 in Kensington Palace in London. Her name was Alexandrina Victoria. When Princess Victoria was 18 years old, her uncle King William died and she became queen. She was crowned at Westminster Abbey in 1838. Victoria married her cousin Albert, a young prince from Germany. Albert didn't speak English very well and lots of people didn't like him. Albert was responsible for such things as the Great Exhibition of 1851.

Victorian timeline

1830   King George dies; William IV becomes king.

1834   The Poor Law Amendment Act says that only the poor who enter a workhouse will be given help. They have to do work for little more than board and lodging.

1837   William IV dies and his niece Victoria becomes queen at age 18.

1838   *Oliver Twist*, by Charles Dickens, is published and shows contrasting conditions of rich and poor.

1840   Queen Victoria marries Prince Albert.

1840   There are 2,100 km of railway line in Britain.

1841   Great Britain has 18.5 million people; Ireland 8 million.

1842   The Mines Act is introduced by Lord Shaftesbury. This stops women and children under 10 from working underground in mines.

1844   The Railways Act makes railway travel possible for all by requiring all lines to offer at least one train a day where the maximum fare is 1p a mile. It also allows the government to take over all railways in times of emergency.

1845–8 Potato famine in Ireland causes many Irish to emigrate and at the same time allows cheap food to arrive from overseas.

1847   The first Factory Act limits the working hours of women and children to 10 hours a day. Chloroform is used as an anaesthetic for the first time.

1848   The Public Health Act sets up boards to oversee public health across the country.

1851   The Great Exhibition takes place – Britain displays her greatness to the world.

1853   Hypodermic syringe invented by Alexander Wood.

Compulsory vaccination against smallpox in Britain.

1854   The first working men's college is set up to help adults improve their education.

1855   Florence Nightingale goes to nurse soldiers injured in fighting and begins her battle against disease.

1859   Samuel Smiles publishes the book *Self-help*, a book which shows how helping yourself in business can lead to greater prosperity. It becomes the 'bible' of the middle classes. Charles Darwin publishes his book *The Origin of Species by Natural Selection*. It will change the way people think about living things.

1860   The Adulteration of Food Act tries to stop bad food from being sold.

1861   Prince Albert dies of typhoid.

1862   The Peabody Trust is founded by banker George Peabody. It will build model houses and blocks of apartments for the poor.

1863   First underground railway built in London. It uses steam trains.

1865   The Sewage Act is passed. It sets up authorities to build sewage works for the first time.

Elizabeth Garrett Anderson becomes the first qualified woman doctor.

1868   An Act is passed to allow local authorities to demolish housing that is unfit for use as homes.

1870   Education Act makes school compulsory for children aged 5–10.

Dr Barnardo opens first home for poor boys in East End. Transportation to Australia for criminals ends.

1871   British population is 26 million; Ireland 5.4 million (2.6 million fewer people than it had in 1841).

The first official public holidays are called Bank Holidays because banks are forced to close.

1875   The telephone is invented by Alexander Graham Bell.

1876   Queen Victoria is proclaimed Empress of India.

1879   Sir John Swan in England and Thomas Edison in the USA both invent the electric light.

1880   There are 28,800 km of railroad track in Britain.

1882   A newspaper makes history by paying women the same wages as men.

1887   Britain celebrates Queen Victoria's Golden Jubilee – her 50th year on the throne.

1888   The first electric power station is opened, allowing electricity to be fed to wealthy homes.

The Football League is founded.

1891   Elementary education is made free for all.

1894   The first motor car is driven in Britain.

1895   The National Trust is formed.

1896   The *Daily Mail* is founded. This is the first newspaper intended to be bought by the lower classes.

1897   Britain celebrates Queen Victoria's Diamond Jubilee – her 60th year on the throne.

1900   The Labour Party is founded.

1901   Queen Victoria dies.

Glossary

ACT OF PARLIAMENT The name for a law passed by the British Parliament.

ANTISEPTIC A chemical that kills bacteria.

BOATER A straw hat, often with a ribbon tied around it.

BRITISH EMPIRE The lands of the world that were ruled by Britain. The British Empire reached its greatest extent during Victorian times.

BUSTLE A frame or pad that caused a skirt to stick out at the hips. Bustles were fashionable in women's dress from around 1870 to 1890.

CENSUS An official count of the population of a country.

CHOLERA A disease caused by drinking water or eating food contaminated by a kind of bacteria. In 1849, some 13,000 people died in an outbreak of cholera in Victorian London. The introduction of sewers and better water supplies helped make such tragedies a thing of the past in Britain.

CLASS A group of people who have the same level of wealth or who move in the same circle.

COMMISSION A group of officials who are given a special task – for example, investigating child labour.

COPYBOOK A school exercise book used for practising handwriting.

CORSET A stiff, tight piece of underwear worn by Victorian women around the upper part of the body to give them a narrow waist.

EXPLOIT To take advantage of other people, often to make money out of them.

GEORGIAN The period in British history before the Victorian age, named after the four King Georges who reigned from 1714 to 1830.

GOVERNESS A women employed by a wealthy family to teach their children at home.

INDUSTRIAL REVOLUTION A period, beginning in the 18th century and finishing in Victorian times, when machines and mass-production began to take over from the hand-making of goods.

MASS-PRODUCTION The making of goods – for example cutlery or cloth – using machinery rather than by handcrafted methods. This was one of the innovations of the Industrial Revolution and enabled factories to produce large quantities of cheap goods.

MEWS A narrow alley behind a terrace of large houses where carriages were kept and horses stabled.

MUSIC HALL A theatre-like place of entertainment where singers, comedians, and dancers performed.

PARISH The smallest area of local government in Britain. Most parishes contain just one or two villages.

PIER A walkway, usually made out of iron, that extends out across the sea. The Victorians built numerous piers in seaside resorts around the country.

PROMENADE A paved pathway by the sea, used by Victorians for seaside walks.

PUBLIC HOUSE A tavern containing a bar and public rooms and designed as a place where people can drink and socialise.

SAFETY BICYCLE Early forms of bicycle had used wooden frames and were so uncomfortable and dangerous that they were called boneshakers. By the late 1870s and 80s, new bicycles using metal frames and rubber tyres were being developed. These were much safer and were so named safety bicycles.

SEWER A pipe that takes dirty water away from homes.

SLUM A dirty, overcrowded house or neighbourhood.

SUBURBS A part of a city which consists almost entirely of housing and shops, and where there are almost no factories or offices.

TELEGRAPH A device for sending messages over distance using electric impulses. The first practical telegraph was invented in Britain in 1837.

TENEMENTS An apartment building, or block of flats, built to extremely low standards and in which people lived in very cramped conditions.

TIED COTTAGE A cottage rented to a worker by his employer as part of his terms of work. When the worker left or was sacked from his job, he lost the right to stay in the cottage.

TRAM Electrically powered vehicles that run along tracks in the road. The first British trams were opened in London and Birkenhead in 1860.

VACCINE A drug that innoculates the body against a disease.

VICTORIANS People who lived during the reign of Queen Victoria; that is, from 1837 to 1901.

WORKHOUSE A place where the poor were given food and shelter in return for labour. In early Victorian times, under the Poor Law Amendment Act of 1834, workhouses became virtual prisons for the poor and were infamous for their harsh conditions. Workhouse conditions improved in late Victorian times.

Index